POLAR BEARS

ROBBIE BYERLY

GINA CLINE

TABLE OF CONTENTS

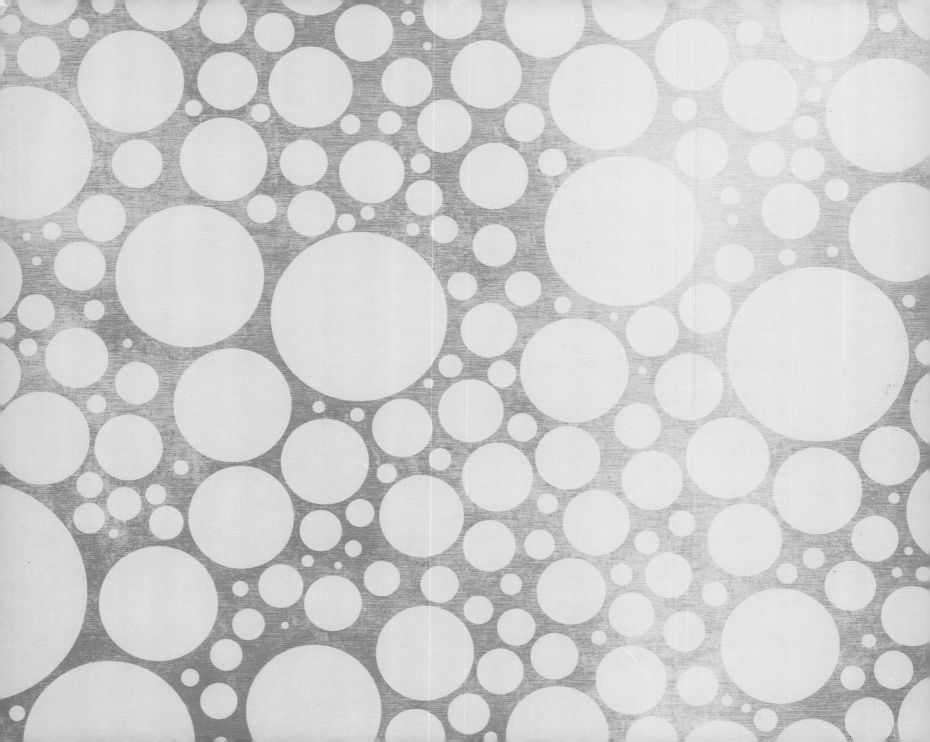

This is a polar bear.

This is a polar bear baby.

This is a polar bear mom.

Baby bears live with the mom.

The mom has 1 or 2 babies.

CAMOUFLAGE

Polar bears look like where they live.

Polar bears look like the snow.

Polar bears look like the ice.

Polar bears look like the rocks.

Polar bears look like the water.

Polar bears have to eat.

Polar bears will eat fish.

Polar bears will eat deer.

Polar bears will eat rabbits.

Polar bears will eat trash.

Polar bears can eat berries.

Polar bears can eat grass.

Polar bears can eat seaweed.

Polar bears can eat whales.

Polar bears love to eat seals.

Polar bears eat lots of seals.

The seal is in the water.

The polar bear is on the ice.

The seal will come up.

The polar bear will get the seal.

POLAR BEARS LIVE HERE

NORTH AMERICA

EUROPE

ASIA

AFRICA

SOUTH
AMERICA

AUSTRALIA

ANTARCTICA

POLAR BEAR BODY PARTS

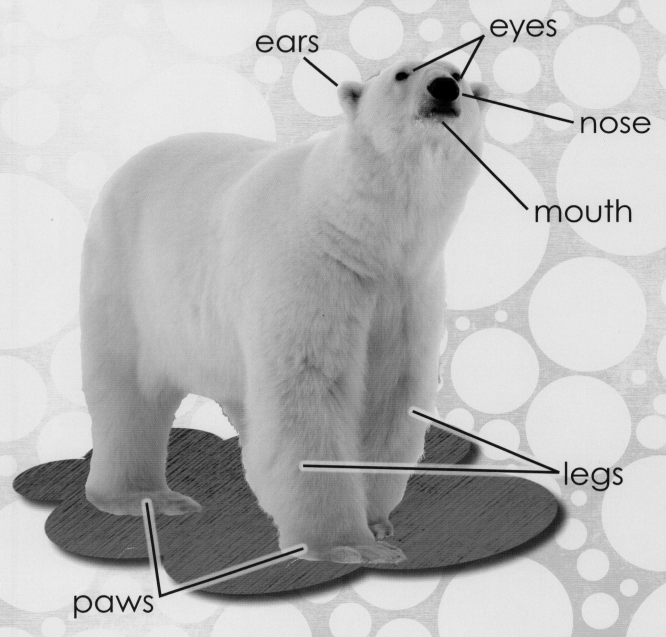

ears

eyes

nose

mouth

legs

paws

THE POLAR BEAR'S FOOD WEB

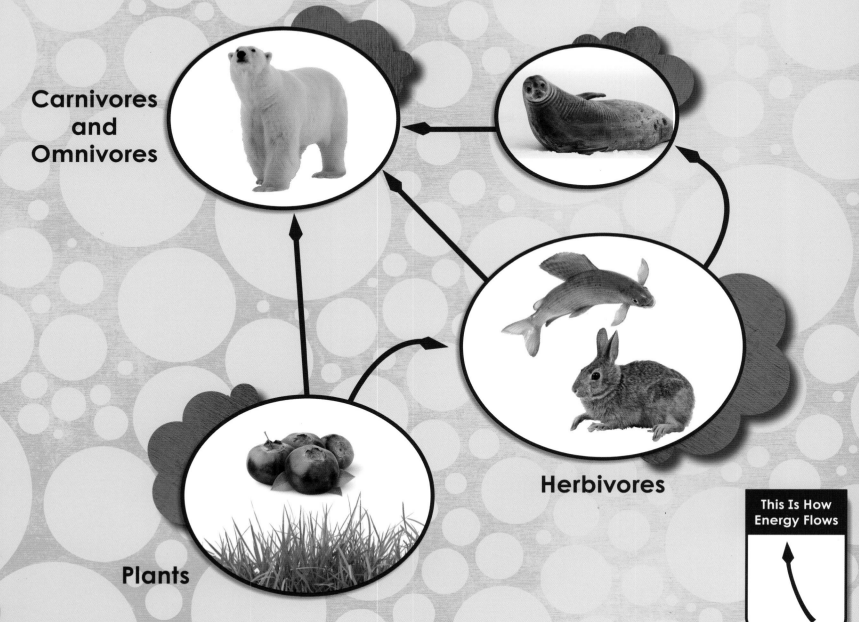

Carnivores and Omnivores

Herbivores

Plants

This Is How Energy Flows

THE POLAR BEAR'S LIFE CYCLE

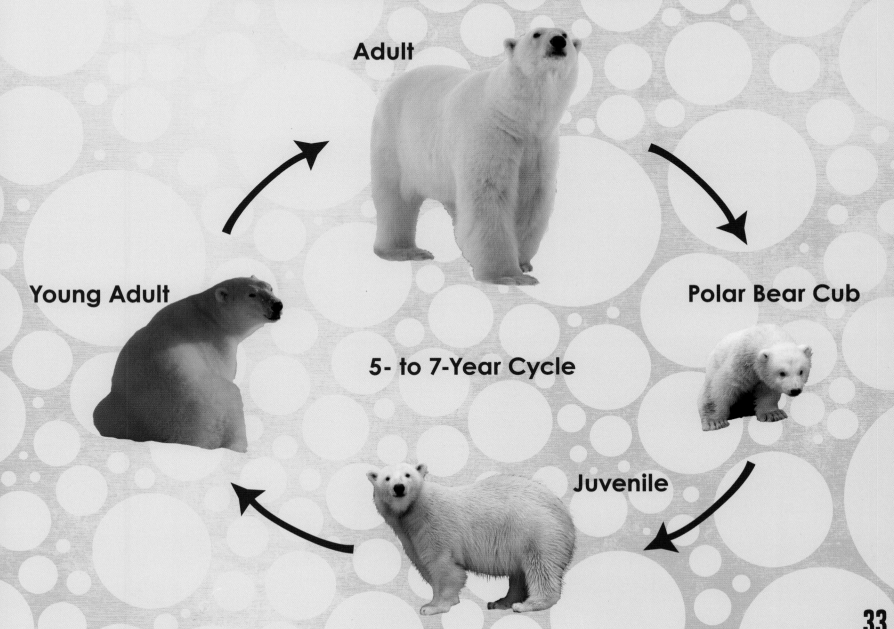

Adult

Young Adult

Polar Bear Cub

5- to 7-Year Cycle

Juvenile

GLOSSARY

POLAR found near the Earth's poles or the area inside the Arctic (North Pole) or Antarctic (South Pole) Circles

SEAL carnivorous marine mammal that mostly lives in cold oceans and has adapted to be a fast swimmer

SEAWEED different kinds of red, green, or brown algae that grow in shallow water and can look like long blades of grass

INDEX

POWER WORDS
HOW MANY CAN YOU READ?

a	has	like	love	they	where
can	have	live	of	this	will
come	in	look	on	to	with
get	is	lots	the	up	